IMAGES
of America

ELIZABETH PARK

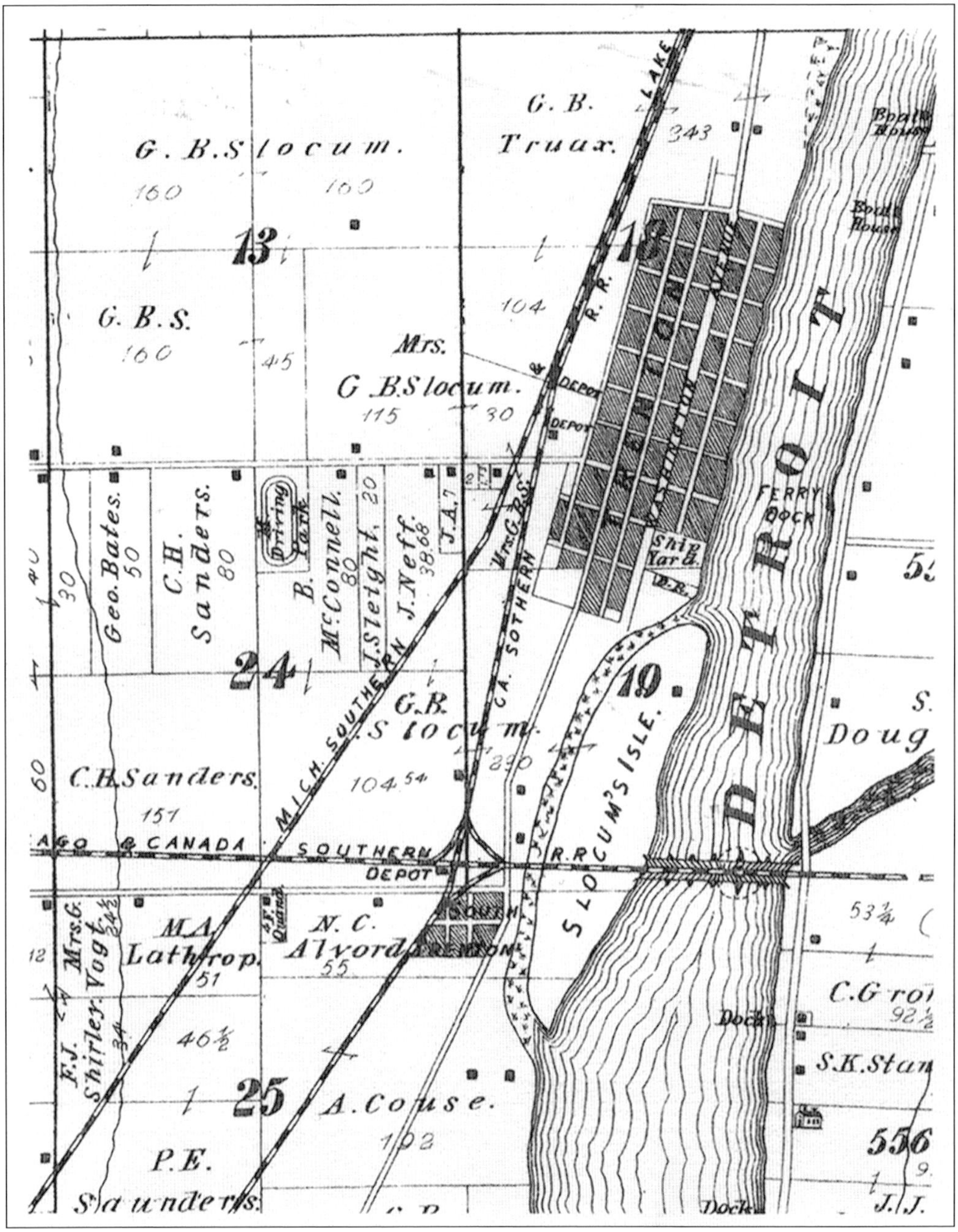

This map of Monguagon Township shows Slocum Island, the village of Trenton to the north, and Grosse Ile to the east. The park's southern boundary extended to the railroad and west to the roadway. The small square near the northern point of the island represents the Slocum house. (Author's collection.)

ON THE COVER: Merry-go-rounds were popular with youngsters. One was located near the Tourist Lodge, and the one pictured was on the island. They were balanced, and usually one child could rotate his or her onboard friends. (Courtesy of Wayne County Road Commission.)

IMAGES
of America

ELIZABETH PARK

Jeff Wagar

ARCADIA
PUBLISHING

ISBN 978-1-4671-0352-7

Published by Arcadia Publishing
Charleston, South Carolina

Printed in the United States of America

Library of Congress Control Number: 2019938112

For all general information, please contact Arcadia Publishing:
Telephone 843-853-2070
Fax 843-853-0044
E-mail sales@arcadiapublishing.com
For customer service and orders:
Toll-Free 1-888-313-2665

Visit us on the Internet at www.arcadiapublishing.com

To those who make a difference.

Contents

Acknowledgments

I wish to thank friends who have urged, even badgered, me into writing this book. And yes, you were right, this has been a fun and rewarding project. Thank you for your persistence.

I further wish to thank the Wayne County Road Commission (WCRC) for its foresight to photographically document the history of the park. All photographs are courtesy of WCRC unless otherwise stated.

I would also be remiss without mentioning William F. Butler (1859–1941). A lifelong Trenton resident and early Wayne County road commissioner whose encouraging words and efforts helped facilitate the Slocum family gift to the county.

But, most of all, I wish to recognize and thank the descendants of the Slocum/Truax families for gifting their land and family home to the people of Wayne County, and by doing so, making it the first county park in the state of Michigan.

It truly is the gift that keeps on giving!

Introduction

Elizabeth Park lies within the boundaries of the small town of Trenton, Michigan. Located on the shores of the Detroit River, it is protected from the ravages of Lake Erie by Grosse Ile and other smaller islands. Its early economy prospered from lumbering and shipbuilding. It became home to ship captains and sailors who found access to nearby forests ideal for shipbuilding.

Trenton was founded by Abraham C. Truax (1778–1844), an early settler from New York State who established a mercantile business in Detroit. He fought in the War of 1812 and was present when Gen. William Hull surrendered his troops and Detroit to the British. Truax escaped and made his way through Canada and returned to his home state. As the British lost control of the area, Truax returned to Detroit to restart his business. He later sold his interest to John May and moved to Ann Arbor, Michigan, and resided there near the Huron River. It is here his daughter, Sophia, the future wife of Giles B. Slocum, was born.

After the war, large blocks of land became available, and in 1820, Truax purchased a tract bordering the Detroit River. First referred to as Truax's Town, the name later morphed to Truaxton, which was used when the town was first platted in 1834. Truax set about developing his town. He asked business contacts to consider moving their interests to the new town. He built a lumber mill, which attracted lumbermen, teamsters, and ship carpenters to the area. His town was growing and needed a post office and a new name; Truaxton now became Truago. The new name was a simple combination of *Tru*ax and Magu*ago*, a nearby Indian village. Slowly, Truax's new town formed, but it wasn't until a fellow New Yorker arrived, built a dock and a warehouse, and married Sophia that the town started to become a reality. Steamers now made regular stops for passengers and goods. Sadly, Abraham Truax never lived to see his town blossom. He was mortally wounded in 1844 when the steamer *General Vance* exploded while approaching the wharf at Sandwich, Ontario, and died later that day.

Truax's son-in-law Giles B. Slocum, already a man of some means, helped continue the Truax dream. Although land records are incomplete for that era, it appears that sometime between his marriage to Sophia Truax in 1838 and events recorded in land records from 1856 that Slocum acquired the property that eventually became Elizabeth Park. Here, he constructed a large wood-frame home and raised his family. His children were educated by Reverend Hunter at his private school on nearby Grosse Ile. That building still exists and can be viewed by standing at the foot of Elm Street in Trenton and looking across the river. (It is the building with the large cupola.)

Slocum was a shrewd and savvy investor known for his honesty. As he and his family prospered, his influence in the area and state grew. Truago grew and was incorporated in 1855 under the name Trenton, honoring the Revolutionary War battle.

Throughout the region and state, Slocum constructed bridges and docks and at one point was given vast timber rights as payment. He died on his island on January 26, 1884. He was survived by his wife, Sophia; son, Elliott Truax Slocum; and daughter, Elizabeth Truax Slocum Nichols.

The Slocum family moved to Detroit but kept the family homestead as a summer residence. Upon the death of Elliott T. Slocum (1839–1915), the island property was offered to the City of Detroit for park purposes. Elliott Slocum had served on Detroit's park commission while developing Belle Isle, and to the benefit of Trenton and Wayne County, Detroit refused the family offer.

Upon hearing of their refusal, Trenton resident and Wayne County Road Commission member William F. Butler urged the family to again make their offer but this time to Wayne County. Among the stipulations, a five-acre parcel bordering the Michigan Central Railway track (today's Grosse Ile Parkway) was to be reserved and given to the Township of Monguagon. This parcel was never granted but rather traded for a small parcel of property in Trenton known as Slocum/Truax Park. This park property became home to a new school, Slocum Truax High School. It graduated its first class in 1924 and its last in 1956. The property has now been restored to a park.

On October 28, 1919, the Slocum family proposal was presented, and the county board accepted the offer the following day. Among the requirements stipulated by the family were that the small, swampy creek encircling the island be widened to a width of 60 feet and that the proposed park be named "Elizabeth" in honor and remembrance of Elizabeth T. Slocum Nichols (1848–1917). Elizabeth Park was officially dedicated July 4, 1923. This book commemorates the 100th anniversary of the Slocum family's generous gift.

One

Slocum Island

The Slocum family had been gracious and generous in allowing public use of their property. They permitted picnickers, campers, baseball games, and holiday celebrations on a limited basis. Occasionally, the family would become upset when chickens were stolen or visitors left behind trash, and they would threaten closure to all. However, all would soon be overlooked, and their property would remain open for public enjoyment.

The family gifting their island property to the county was not only generous but involved great foresight to a changing and evolving society. At the time, the work week was six days. The gift allowed families and visitors to spend a memorable day together, to picnic and participate in the new park's many available activities. Here, a visitor could choose from shuffleboard, horseshoes, tennis, baseball, buggy rides, boat rides, bicycling, canoeing, and a children's wading pool. Also, the Slocum Recreation House provided checkers, dominoes, card games, and table tennis. Of course, there were many tables and stoves available throughout the grounds for cookouts. For the traveler, the Tourist Lodge provided campsites and other amenities.

The park gift consisted of approximately 156 acres and was not really an island until a marshy area was dredged into a 4,800-foot-by-60-foot canal in 1925.

This early postcard, dated 1907, shows Slocum Island's shoreline as viewed from the Detroit River. To the left is the pathway from the Slocum house leading to the shoreline boathouse and dock. In the background at right are several homes located in the village of Trenton.

In the view on this postcard looking south from the village of Trenton to Slocum Island, the remnants of the Turner Shipyard and original entrance to the island are shown. The road is now known as Riverside Drive and leads to a footbridge entrance to the park. The Slocum and caretaker houses are partially hidden by the woods. Faintly seen in the background along the river is the railroad bridge that marked the southern border of the park.

Slocum Island was rural and rustic. Much of the property was unimproved except the section on the mainland where farming was conducted. After the death of Giles B. Slocum, the family made several improvements. One of the improvements was a small road (shown here) that led to the southern end of the island. Footpaths were made where family, guests, and other visitors could walk secluded paths along the riverbank and other areas. (Courtesy of Claude Owen.)

Claude Owen and family members are enjoying a moment together at the Slocum dock. Owen, who was a druggist in Trenton, is at left. He became a member of the Trenton School Board and was later honored with the Claude Owen Elementary School named for him. (Courtesy of Claude Owen.)

This was the view from West Jefferson Avenue looking toward Slocum Island. Shown in the foreground is the land that was farmed for the family. (Courtesy of Claude Owen.)

Shown in this photograph dated 1915 is one of the secluded pathways that could be found on the island before Wayne County took control. (Courtesy of Claude Owen.)

Of the several small streams that could be found on the island, some became streams only after heavy periods of rain. These steams provided moisture that added to the lushness and variety for both walks and wild flowers. Springtime visitors to the island sometimes reported that the mosquito population was unbearable. (Courtesy of Claude Owen.)

This postcard, dated 1911, shows an adult, two children, and a dog pausing from their walk to have their photograph taken. The path bordered the Detroit River south of the Slocum residence. The Grosse Ile shoreline can be seen across the river.

Pictured is a view of the original entrance to Slocum Island looking north from the island toward the village of Trenton. From this location, the road turned east to the Slocum residence. The small wooden bridge at center crossed the stream and a marshy area that Wayne County later dredged and widened. (Courtesy of Claude Owen.)

Here is a closer view of the wooden entrance bridge. The road continued north to a roadway then named Front Street, now called Riverside Drive. The tower shown at the right was located at the foot of St. Joseph Avenue and Riverside Drive and was the source of water for the village of Trenton.

For many years, the Slocum house was the finest in Trenton. This is the west-side view of the home. Built by Giles B. Slocum around the Civil War period, the home is first recorded on an 1876 map of Monguagon Township. It was well maintained and remained in the family even after Slocum's death in 1884. The family relocated to Detroit and maintained the house as a summer residence, often visiting for weekends and holidays. As the driveway approached the house, it turned, continuing to the right to a nearby carriage house/barn. The stone entrance pillars were milled locally at the Sibley Quarry. When Wayne County acquired the property, the house was renovated into a community recreation building. Inside, visitors could play Ping-Pong, checkers, dominoes, and cards. Sadly, the home was lost to arson in 1975. (Claude Owen.)

The Slocum caretaker's house sat to the south and west of the residence, facing the roadway to the island. The Laatz family lived there for a short time as caretakers. Mr. Laatz had been injured working the Slocum farm. John Brow and his family were the last residents of the house while it was still located on the island. As Wayne County worked to develop plans for Elizabeth Park, county officials hired Brow to oversee the island and provide security for the property. Besides his salary, he was allowed use of the home rent free. Wayne County later offered the house to anyone willing to pay the cost of relocating it off the island. Nick Mans, a Trenton resident, moved the house to a lot on the east side of Elizabeth Drive, where it sits today. (Courtesy of Claude Owen.)

This 1914 postcard shows just how crowded and popular Slocum's Island was for visitors. This is the original roadway to the island. In the view looking south, adults and children are strolling and enjoying what looks to be a fine spring day.

The Canadian Southern Railway bridge marks the southern boundary of the park property. The Michigan Central line later acquired the Canadian Southern, and the bridge was removed and replaced with a new swing bridge, constructed by the Wayne County Road Commission in the early 1930s. A five-acre parcel of property adjoining the north side of the bridge right-of-way was gifted to Monguagon Township. The township later traded this property for a small park parcel that had been previously donated to the village by the Slocums. Located in Trenton near Third Street and Harrison, it became the site for a new, much-needed high school. The new school was named the Slocum-Truax High School and graduated its first class in 1924 and the last in 1956. The building then was used as a junior high school and was demolished in the 1980s. The property reverted to the original small park, known once again as Slocum-Truax Park. (Courtesy of Claude Owen.)

Use of the island was popular with both individuals and groups. Here, in 1916, the local Damascus Society is shown camping and relaxing near the Detroit River shoreline. (Courtesy of Claude Owen.)

Camping was not without chores. Laundry and drying wet clothes from a dip in the river were necessary and common. (Courtesy of Claude Owen.)

Rev. Roy G. Hershey, from the Trenton Presbyterian Church, is shown camping with an early group of Trenton Boy Scouts in 1914. In the fall of that year, Reverend Hershey left Trenton to accept another assignment in Ithaca, Michigan. (Courtesy of Claude Owen.)

The village of Trenton's town baseball club was known as the Seminoles. The club contacted the Slocum family in 1895, asking and receiving permission to construct a baseball diamond on the island. The Seminoles were disbanded when the Trenton schools began fielding their own baseball team. The new school team played its games on the island until a field was prepared at the new high school. Seminole team members named in this undated photograph are Mr. Hoggard, Hinch, Baker, and E. Ouellette. (Courtesy of Claude Owen.)

This view looking north from the Michigan Central Railroad line where it crosses West Jefferson Avenue shows the mainland property of the island and the future site of the proposed Tourist Lodge.

This rare photograph of the Slocum carriage house shows Edna Brown of Brownstown Township sitting on a horse. The carriage house was located south of the Slocum house, east of the caretaker's house, and was demolished to make way for the construction of the new North Comfort Station. (Courtesy of Ken Brown.)

Two

A Gift for Park Purposes

For many years, there were rumors and statements about the provisions of the Slocum family's donation of the land that was to become Elizabeth Park. One such rumor was that because of Elliott Slocum's work for Detroit's Belle Ile park board and, at one time, the family offering their land to Detroit, the City of Detroit could seize Elizabeth Park for its own. But Detroit refused the family offer and had no further claims.

Another misconception came about pertaining to the property after the death of Elliott T. Slocum in 1915. In fact, he did bequeath the island property to the Township of Monguagon. The only problem was, he did not own it. Ownership was shared with his sister, Elizabeth Slocum Nichols, who survived him. The courts ruled the property was hers by right of survivorship. Later, she made the offer of gifting the land to Detroit in memory of her brother, which Detroit politely refused. Then entered Trenton resident and Wayne County Road Commission board member William F. Butler. He persuaded the family to again consider donating their land, but this time to Wayne County to be used as a park.

In a letter to the Wayne County Board of Supervisors, Elliot S. Slocum wrote:

> This land is offered on condition that it be accepted and maintained in perpetuity by the County as a public park to be known as Elizabeth Park. Furthermore, that the County establish in the park suitable playgrounds and facilities for the use of the park by the public and make the necessary improvements for this purpose. For the purpose of properly improving the land for park purposes it will be necessary to construct a canal through the low ground between the island and the mainland, the canal to be sixty feet or more in width and to extend from the Detroit River to the right of way of the Canada Southern Railway, the banks of the canal to be properly graded back so as to fill the remainder of the low ground. This gift is offered upon the above conditions and with the hope that the County will accept the gift and carry out the intentions of the donors to create in memory of Elizabeth Slocum Nichols, a public park permanently devoted to the wholesome amusement and outdoor recreation.

The City of Trenton has made several attempts to gain control and ownership of the park. Its efforts have all been rebuffed.

In 1921, crews began to clear and rough grade the park's circular drive. Work continued throughout the winter to take advantage of the frozen ground.

During the summer of 1922, crews worked pouring concrete. An early on-site cement mixer and concrete leveling bar are shown in operation.

This photograph, dated 1922, shows batch cars and a mixer in operation. Each car was loaded with the necessary amount of sand, stone, and cement used to mix concrete. As the cars were emptied, the track was taken up and placed at the opposite end.

This postcard offers a view of the Slocum house before its renovation by Wayne County. The porches were made larger, and the second floor was converted to public restrooms. Later, the first-floor interior walls were removed and remodeled as a Community Recreation House. In 1924, a first-aid station with nurse was established, and in 1927, the second floor was again remodeled, this time as an infirmary.

The firm of Dunbar and Sullivan of Troy, New York, was contracted to create the canal stipulated by the Slocum gift. Here, the company's machine nicknamed "Big Dipper" is seen in a 1923 photograph placing some of the excavated material to fill the shoreline adjacent to the Detroit River.

The first of the comfort stations was constructed near the site of the Slocum carriage house. Named the North Comfort Station, it was demolished due to vandalism in the early 2000s.

The Grand Entrance to the park was completed in 1922. This photograph, dated 1930, has a view looking north from the park toward the village of Trenton. The small informational booth at the left was manned and enabled the county to keep an accurate traffic count of visitors.

Paving of the circle drive, completed in 1922, is shown in this photograph dated 1924. Entering traffic went to the right. Later, a larger one-way sign was installed that alleviated confusion for drivers.

In 1923, Trenton resident John Clyde Winnie was hired as the first park guard with a salary of $150 a month. On June 20, he handed out the first ticket. It was a speeding ticket issued to Ed Soncrant, who was fined $5 and $2.50 court cost.

In 1923, the park added baseball diamonds. They were immediately popular and park maintenance crews had difficulty keeping grass on the fields.

Two baseball diamonds are seen here with a new planting of grass. The wooden structure in the background at right is the original park concession stand that was operated by James Ferguson. A permanent brick replacement was built in 1930, and the temporary stand was moved to the corner of West Jefferson Avenue and Walnut Street in Trenton. It was later opened as the first A&W in Michigan, at first selling only root beer and popcorn. It was owned by Pete Duich.

There is nothing better than playing baseball with a view of the Detroit River and enjoying the cooling breeze. By 1924, the fields had become so popular that reservations were required.

Shoreline stabilization was completed by the firm of Dunbar and Sullivan. The placing of fill allowed the park to construct a dock for excursion rides and create additional picnicking areas. The walkway led from the circle drive to the waterfront. In this 1924 view looking upriver toward the village of Trenton are the park boat dock and, in the distance, the Purdy Boat Company.

This 1924 photograph shows the park shoreline looking south, downriver toward the Michigan Central Railroad bridge where it crosses the Detroit River. It provides a visible marker to the southern boundary of the park property. The smokestacks, partially hidden by the trees, mark the home of the newly constructed Detroit Edison Trenton Channel Plant.

In 1928, the Detroit Speed Boat Livery operated a boat ride concession from the boat dock. Delbert Lockhart started a ferry service to nearby Grosse Ile utilizing the dock. In 1932, a three-year boat ride concession was granted to Harry J. Bureau. Shown is the *Major Wilcox* leaving the dock. The cost was 10¢ for a 20-minute ride. This was a popular attraction, helping drive park attendance to over 900,000 visitors.

The excursion boat *DYC III* was operated by the Holden family of Trenton, Michigan. *DYC* was short for the Detroit Yacht Club. The boat is pictured in this post–World War II photograph.

Shown here is the landscaped boat dock with the excursion boat leaving for a ride upriver in 1936. Across the river is the shoreline of Grosse Ile. The ornate lighting was installed by Detroit Edison.

Construction proceeds on one of three pedestrian bridges connecting the park to the mainland in 1924. This is the bridge located behind the Tourist Lodge.

By 1925, the canal had been widened and deepened as stipulated by the Slocum gift. Seen from the new park entrance looking toward the Detroit River, the Slocum house is visible among the trees next to the North Comfort Station. Shoreline walkways and ornate lighting ring the waterfront. For safety, emergency life-rings were placed along the shore.

Boats enjoying the canal passage were often seen tied up along the canal banks with passengers enjoying a picnic lunch or other park activities.

In response to requests from park visitors, a drinking fountain pavilion was constructed in 1925. The location chosen was north of the boat dock near picnicking and playground areas.

To meet the needs of park patrons, two additional comfort stations were added, as shown here in 1925. The East Comfort Station site was chosen for its proximity to the tennis courts and future planned wading pool. The West Comfort Station location was chosen for use in the western, more remote, picnicking sites and bicycle rental locations shown in the 1925 photograph below.

During the winter of 1925, Wayne County employees plant trees and landscape the entrance road to Elizabeth Park. They are near the corner of West Jefferson Avenue and Walnut Street. The county policy was to beautify roadsides by planting trees.

Shown in these 1929 photographs are the four tennis courts that were constructed in 1922. The courts were in demand for many years, and the local high schools practiced and played matches here on occasion. Tennis is still among the most popular sports at the park.

The park was popular for picnicking. The above photograph shows a family reunion in 1928. Below, picnickers at tables and a large crowd are shown watching a baseball game near the newly completed concession stand in 1930.

The temporary wooden concession stand was relocated to the corner of West Jefferson Avenue and Walnut Street in the village of Trenton. Owned by Pete Duich, the stand became home to the first A&W in the state of Michigan and is shown here in 1952. (Courtesy of Agnes Duich.)

This aerial photograph of the Detroit River, with Grosse Ile to the right and Elizabeth Park to the left, was taken during the 1931 dedication of the new Trenton–Grosse Ile Bridge. The walled-off area in the water along the shoreline north of the bridge is the proposed sheltered swim beach. Water for the swim area was to be filtered and chlorinated by a turbine-driven pump. It was never built, and this later became the site for long-term boat dockage.

Children are enjoying a teeter-totter that overlooked the Detroit River. It was a popular activity for many years, as seen in this 1930 photograph.

Children are having fun on swing sets that were once located south of the Community House. They also enjoyed a view overlooking the river, as seen in this 1930 photograph. Today's park still has several of the original swing sets in use.

These two photographs, taken in 1925 (above) and 1930, show the staging area and hitching rail for the pony and buggy concession. It has been a very popular activity throughout the years; however, only pony rides are now offered.

Soon after the nearly three-quarter-mile pony trail was completed, visitors could take an escorted pony ride or drive a one- or two-person buggy, as shown in these photographs from 1925 and 1927. The trail runs through a wooded area inside the park's circular roadway and deliberately meanders, giving the rider a feeling of being alone on the trail.

Shown here in 1925 is a youngster riding a pony accompanied by an attendant. Not far from this location, the trail bends to the left and the concession staging area can be seen by both pony and rider. Ponies usually increased their pace here, eager to return to the hitch stand.

In 1925, F.R. Watkins was granted a five-year pony ride concession. In 1928, a Pony Barn was constructed in the center of the pony trail, not far from the concession staging area. Ponies could then be stabled and fed on-site, as seen in this 1929 photograph.

In 1926, a new Shelter Building, located south of the boat dock overlooking the Detroit River, was completed. It housed an area for indoor picnicking and one for shuffleboard, and a southern wing for park maintenance equipment.

The rear of the Shelter Building, sitting high on the riverbank, afforded park visitors a view of the river, with cooling breezes in the summer. Downstream offered a view of the railroad bridge and trains, and a look upriver provided a view of the village of Trenton and beyond.

Shown is a view of the pavilion/veranda at the rear of the Shelter Building. Here, visitors could relax in settees and rocking chairs and enjoy the view and refreshing breezes from the river.

This 1928 photograph of the interior of the center section of the Shelter Building shows its original setup. Later, the picnic tables were removed and replaced with shuffleboard courts.

The southern wing of the Shelter Building is where park maintenance equipment was parked, maintained, and stored. The rear of the building contained a coal-fired boiler that provided both heat and hot water to the structure. A small office and lockers were behind the boiler, and the double doors seen at left provided access to the other wings, as seen in this 1929 photograph.

This is a ground-floor view of the equipment wing looking toward the front of the Shelter Building. It shows a small workbench and storage area on the left; another unseen workbench and area is to the right of the scene in this 1929 photograph.

This 1929 photograph taken facing the rear of the building shows the upstairs storage area for the equipment wing. The park guard's motorcycle is stored for the winter.

This opposite view was also taken in 1929, facing the front of the Shelter Building. The cantilevered upstairs storage floor is supported by the roof structure.

The new concession stand pictured here was built in 1930 and operated by Chris Vlachols, who met patrons' needs with snacks and cool drinks. It replaced the wooden temporary stand operated by James Furguson that would later become the first A&W in Michigan.

Tourist Lodge and Camp was one of the first county-operated campgrounds in the country. The lodge was located on West Jefferson Avenue on the mainland section of the park. It was dedicated

by Edward Hines on June 15, 1925.

These two views show the available camping areas. They contained 150 campsites, 50 with tables, stoves, and running water. The cost was 50¢ a day, with a maximum three-day stay. Gas rationing during World War II wiped out the camping industry, and the lodge was remodeled into a restaurant and concession stand.

The interior of the Tourist Lodge was equipped with restrooms, coin-operated showers costing 10¢, and a dining room with cooking stoves operated with gas supplied by a generator housed in the basement. Another small room acted as a concession stand that was stocked with canned goods and charcoal and had a telephone and mailbox. Laundry tubs and clothes irons were placed in the basement for convenience. A covered concrete pad was outside to the rear of the building. Here, motorists had an air pump for tire repairs. Another indoor room served as a lounge area and was outfitted with desks and seats. It had a fireplace where visitors could relax and read or write letters about their travel adventures.

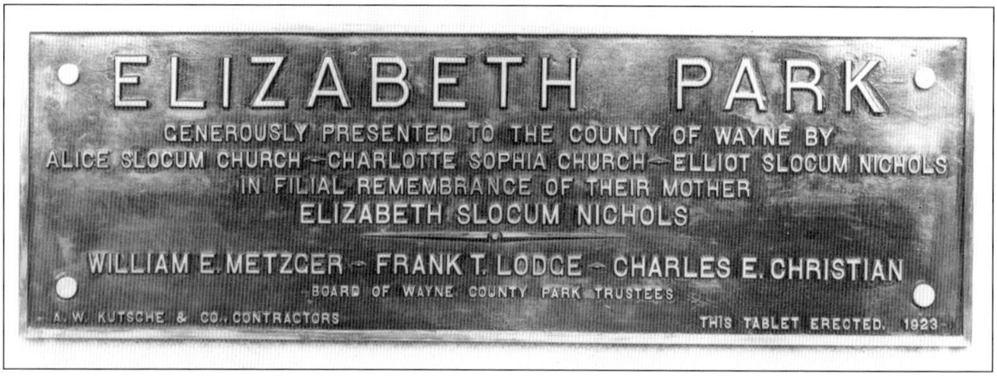

This dedication plaque was located at the Grand Entrance to the park. The Slocum gift to the county was in 1919, but the official dedication was July 4, 1923.

Three comfort stations were positioned in the park to provide easy access and convenience for visitors. All were constructed between 1925 and 1929. Today, only the West Comfort Station remains.

This is a view looking north on West Jefferson Avenue approaching the Tourist Lodge. Shown is the finish grading to the roadway being completed. West Jefferson was one of the earliest roads in Michigan and was built to allow the transportation of troops and supplies between Detroit and Monroe during the War of 1812.

The Drinking Fountain Pavilion was located near the Community House and was constructed in 1925. The pavilion allowed park visitors to quench their thirst with a refreshing drink of water and was later converted into a second concession stand to keep up with demand. Two additional drinking fountains were installed nearby to compensate for the loss.

The last ornamental footbridge was built east of the main entrance to the park. It was constructed in 1929 on the site of the original family entrance to Slocum Island.

The Central States Rowing Competition, held in August 1929, was the first event to be held at the park. The finish line was at the site of the boat dock. The event attracted large crowds over the two-day regatta.

The rowing event was so well attended it caused parking and traffic problems both on and off the island. These photographs show congestion on the island near the boat dock. State and local police were called upon to direct traffic.

Elizabeth Drive, the entrance road to the park, is shown with police directing traffic. Compounding the congestion is a circus being staged on the vacant property at left.

Crowds came to spend the day watching the events unfold. The overflow crowd took up positions on the Grosse Ile shore opposite the park.

The winner of the regatta was the Wyandotte/Detroit Boat Club.

The hosting town of Trenton entered its own team. With only eight days of practice, and using a borrowed scull, the team finished last. Members of the Trenton team competing in the 1927 race were W.E. Rogers Jr., Arthur Ford, J.W. Armstrong, ? Cottington, Irwin Kemp, Charles Hornauer, Cam Waldorf, Charles Woolnough, and Harold Bolduc.

Ice-skating provided outdoor recreation for park visitors, as shown in this 1936 photograph. Starting out with two rinks, with two more plus a warming shed added later, skating proved popular for many years. The only drawback was that the ice was dependent upon the weather. A posted sign gave notice: "Skating Today" or "No Skating Today."

This 1919 view of the intersection of West Jefferson Avenue and Grosse Ile Parkway faces north. The western and southern borders of Elizabeth Park are to the right, and the Michigan Central railroad track is seen as it crosses West Jefferson, leading to a small train station named Slocum Junction.

Shown are two views of the wading pool that was constructed in 1931. It was located across from the Shelter Building and was a popular spot for cooling off during the warm summer months. Occasionally closing during summer polio season scares, the pool was permanently closed by the Detroit Health Board in the late 1950s. It is now the site of a children's water park.

PLEASE DO NOT

Shown is the Slocum House shortly after it was renovated and remodeled as the Community House. In 1921, the porches were made larger and the second floor converted to public restrooms. A first-aid station was added in 1924. In 1927, the second floor was again remodeled and furnished as an infirmary and staffed with nurses. Initially, the house was open year-round. When the infirmary ceased operations, the facility offered recreational activities on a seasonal basis only.

The Community House was heavily used during the World War II gas rationing years. Photographed in 1942, these two views of the first floor interior show children playing Ping-Pong and checkers. At the checker table are, from left to right, Jack Chesney, Don Chesney, and James Doyle.

This early photograph of West Jefferson Avenue was taken in 1912 near the future site of the Tourist Lodge. This section of road shows the narrow box culverts that caused many sideswiping accidents. Just south of here, at another narrow culvert, were the world's first traffic lines. Center lines were painted on the roadway, allowing approaching vehicles to keep to their side of the road. It proved effective in helping eliminate many of these types of accidents. It worked so well, the lines were later adopted and used throughout the world.

Vandalism continues at the park. Shown are 19 of the 50 picnic tables damaged during the summer of 1983. Park buildings suffered broken windows. Comfort station interiors were damaged as well as concession stand equipment. Due to a lack of funds, repairs were not made, and the park suffered in use and image.

The Community House is shown boarded up and winterized. The building remained shuttered due to lack of use and available funding for its maintenance.

Three

Today's Park

Probably the lowest point in the park's existence was the torching of the old Slocum/Community House in 1975. The house was the visible reminder and connection to the Slocum family, and many park visitors mourned the loss. In 1977, a county-commissioned study estimated the damage to park structures and plantings exceeded $50,000, and this figure did not include the loss of the Slocum/Community House. People responded, calling for action to fund and protect the park. Their efforts took many years, but finally, in 1996, resulted in the approval of a countywide millage dedicated to all Wayne County parks.

Meanwhile, the county tried to interest a noted local restauranteur to develop and convert either the Tourist Lodge or Shelter Building into a restaurant. In 1980, the park received a $50,000 grant, augmented by $12,500 from the county, to stabilize a segment of the shoreline along the Detroit River. A handicapped-accessible ramp and stairway were also added at the same site. In 1981, the Michigan Coastal Management Program awarded the county another $31,000 to construct a fishing pier. Also, the City of Trenton attempted to bill the county $14,000 for costs incurred answering calls to stop rowdiness at the park. Police and county officials recommended closing a segment of the park's circular drive to prevent "looping."

In 1984, the park circle drive was resurfaced with asphalt. Later in the year, the first annual Somewhere in Time event was held. This event, along with other family-type events like the Marshmallow Drop, created in 1986, spur families to return to the park.

With the passage of the countywide park millage, funds became available for renovation and new projects. In 2003, the Roar on the River boat race relocated to Elizabeth Park, and the Southshore Riverwalk dedication was held December 16, 2003. In 2004, construction started on the Elizabeth Park Northpoint section of the riverfront, and renovations began on the Shelter Building and Tourist Lodge. In 2012, Wayne County reached an agreement with the City of Trenton and leased marina operations to the city. In the summer of 2013, work began on demolition and reconstruction of the three park pedestrian bridges.

Here, demolition and removal start on one of the three original park pedestrian bridges. The project began in the summer of 2013 and was completed in the fall. (Author's collection.)

A safety/staging barge was floated and anchored in place. This allowed workers to stand on the barge and work on framing for the bridge arches. (Author's collection.)

A crane is lifting the first of three arch segments. Each of the bridges consisted of three preformed concrete arches. (Author's collection.)

Three arch segments are shown lifted and placed at North Pedestrian Bridge. Next in the installation process was pouring concrete for sides and steps. (Author's collection.)

Workers have finished forming and are now pouring concrete for the sides of the bridge. Later, forms will be put in place for the concrete steps of the bridge. (Author's collection.)

Shown here is the installation of the ornate bridge railing. All that was left were the cleanup and installation of an ornate streetlight. (Author's collection.)

Shown here are two views of the completed Children's Fountain Park. Built at the site of the old wading pool, the Children's Fountain Park is awaiting a water source before being activated. (Both, author's collection.)

The Northshore Project is shown completed in this photograph with a view looking north from the boat dock. The newly restored walkway and stabilized shoreline allowed the construction of two fishing piers. The one seen in the distance is a handicapped-accessible fishing pier jutting out from the shoreline. (Author's collection.)

Funding for many of the recent projects at Elizabeth Park has been provided through grants acquired from oil, gas, and mineral revenue from state-owned lands. There is a similar sign at the western side of the park, near the Tourist Lodge, for the Bicycle Beltway connection. (Author's collection.)

The Shelter Building has been converted to a catering facility for weddings, reunions, and other events. (Author's collection.)

An original double swing set is shown here. There are two other original swing sets located within the park. (Author's collection.)

Constructed in 1925, today's Tourist Lodge is newly renovated and landscaped. The lodge now functions as the park offices. Shown here are the rear and south views of the building. (Author's collection.)

Near the former Tourist Lodge camping sites, a warming shed has been constructed. There are now four skating ponds available during the winter months, weather permitting. (Author's collection.)

Upstream from the kayak launch is one of the renovated footbridges. The graceful arched bridge has provided many photo opportunities to park visitors. (Author's collection.)

Today's view from where the Slocum/Community House once sat gives visitors a panorama of the Detroit River and Grosse Ile. The scene provides a respite from the day's activities. (Author's collection.)

Shown in these two photographs are two of the three newly constructed picnic pavilions. Instead of the earlier concept of dispersed picnic sites, park officials have clustered sheltered picnic areas that provide easier access and aid park maintenance personnel in cleanup. (Both, author's collection.)

Newly completed in 2018, the bicycle/hiking trail connects to a system of joined trails that traverse Wayne County. (Author's collection.)

This sign acknowledges portions of the trail that are paid for with grants derived from the production of oil, gas, and minerals on state-owned lands. (Author's collection.)

Part of the recently added attractions to the park are a series of fitness stations shown here. They are positioned near the entrance to the park, continuing and ending near the West Comfort Station. Each station is designed for a different exercise, helping to maximize the workout. (Both, Author's collection.)

Each fitness station has a sign directing the use and duration of the workout. This station is named the "Chain Balancer." (Author's collection.)

Here is a view of the Chain Balancer station positioned near the end of the course. The sign directs the level of activity for beginners and advanced fitness levels. The sign (mercifully) directs the user to "jog" to the next and final station. (Author's collection.)

Today's Concession Stand did not open for the 2018 season. It is slated to be remodeled and renovated to another proposed purpose, possibly restrooms. (Author's collection.)

Today's pony concession is still located on the same site. However, buggy rides are no longer offered. (Author's collection.)

A boat ramp capable of six launches was first constructed in 1958. The park marina has been upgraded with increased parking and launch sites. Shown is the ticket booth located at the marina entrance. (Author's collection.)

The neon marina sign is attached to the gable of the park offices. (Author's collection.)

Long-term boat dockage was added at the site of the long-ago proposed bathing beach. (Author's collection.)

New handicapped-accessible park offices were added near the boat launch and parking lot. The marina is now operated by the City of Trenton under a lease agreement with Wayne County. (Author's collection.)

Located at the rear of the renovated Shelter Building, the veranda offers a view of the Detroit River. The shoreline of Grosse Ile is seen at the far side of the river. This section of the river is busy with small boat traffic and an occasional freighter delivering coal to Detroit Edison's Trenton Channel Plant. (Author's collection.)

The site of the boat dock is where excursion boats once offered park visitors rides, but increased costs and liability issues caused the rides to become unprofitable. The dock remains, but rides are no longer offered. The dock does get some use during Somewhere in Time events held at the park, when a tour boat offers a guided historical tour of the river. (Author's collection.)

A new kayak launch has been added on the canal behind the Tourist Lodge. A nearby parking lot makes transport to the launch nearly effortless. (Author's collection.)

The kayak launch site features a system designed to make it easy for wheelchair users to enter and exit kayaks and canoes. The site has proven popular, and kayak lessons are offered during the summer. (Author's collection.)

Every Easter, a helicopter brings Santa Claus to the park for the Marshmallow Drop event. Hovering over the baseball field, Santa drops marshmallows to waiting children. The children are given bags to gather as many as they can, and all win a prize. This popular family event was first held in 1986. (Courtesy of Joann Gonyea.)

This little girl is gathering the dropped marshmallows. Unfortunately, most Easters at the park are chilly and damp, but the kids have lots of fun. (Courtesy of Joann Gonyea.)

In the middle of this photograph sits the last connection to the Slocum family, or pre-county, ownership of the island, the Slocum family caretaker's residence. The house sits on the east side of Elizabeth Drive, next to the last house before Slocum Avenue. Wayne County offered the house free to anyone who would move it off the island. Nick Mans, a Trenton resident, moved the house to its present location in 1924. (Author's collection.)

Bibliography

Burton, Clarence M. *Compendium of History and Biography of the City of Detroit and Wayne County, Michigan*. Chicago, IL: H. Taylor & Co., 1909.

Christie, Robert. *The Military and Naval Operations in the Canadas During the Late War with the United States*. New York, NY: Oram and Mott, 1818.

Elizabeth Park Southshore Riverwalk Dedication. December 16, 2003.

Federal Writers Project. *Michigan: A Guide to the Wolverine State*. Somerset Publishers, 1941.

Hull, General William. "Surrender of Detroit." August 16, 1812.

Land Offered as Gift for Park Purposes to the Board of Supervisors, County of Wayne, State of Michigan. Letter from Elliott S. Nichols dated October 28, 1919.

Leake, Paul. *History of Detroit*, Vol. II. Lewis Publishing, 1912.

Leyden, James Alexander. A *Historical Sketch of the Fourth Infantry from 1796 to 1861*. Fort Sherman, ID: Press of the Fourth United States Infantry, 1891.

Palmer, Thomas H. *The Historical Register of the United States. Part II: From the Declaration of War in 1812 to January 1, 1814*. Washington, DC: T.H. Palmer, 1814.

Report of County Park Trustees of Wayne County, Michigan, to the Board of Supervisors of Wayne County, Michigan. December 1, 1919 to September 1, 1923.

Treaty of Chicago, 1821.

Wayne County Parks History Timeline. www.waynecounty.com.

Wayne County Marina Lease Agreement, 2012–2018.

Democratic Free Press. June 25–27, 1844.

Guardian/Herald. November 5, 1975.

Trenton Times. July 23, 1915; October 31, 1919; January 20, 1920; July 20, 1920; July 30, 1920; August 27, 1920; November 4, 1921; November 11, 1921; January 13, 1922; June 23, 1922; August 4, 1922; September 15, 1922; November 17, 1922; December 1, 1922; April 20, 1923; June 8, 1923; June 29, 1923; April 25, 1924; July 4, 1924; August 1, 1924; March 20, 1925; June 19, 1925; April 22, 1927; February 1, 1929; February 4, 1930; October 3, 1930; May 15, 1931; August 7, 1931; February 19, 1932; August 9, 1935; April 24, 1958.

Wyandotte Herald. June 7, 1895; August 23, 1913.

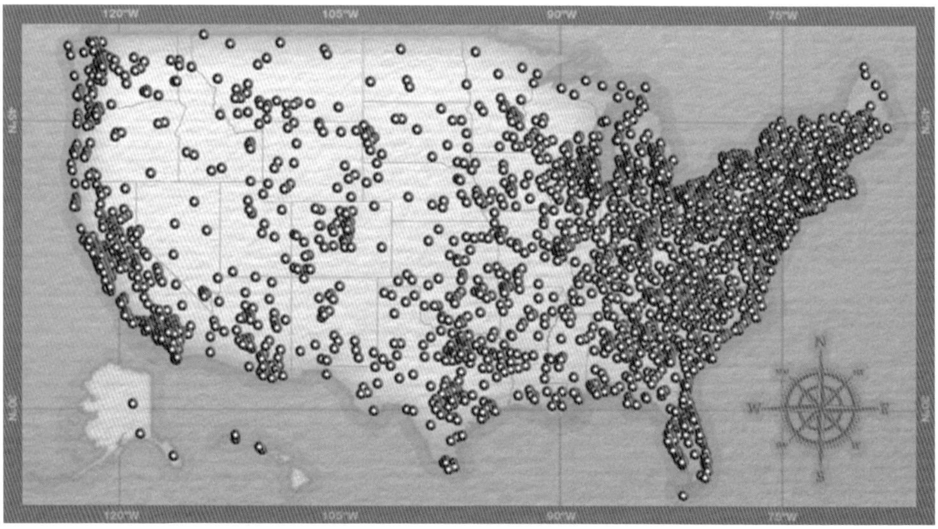